CHEMISTRY

D1099950

KINGFISHER

KINGFISHER

First published 2010 by Kingfisher
This revised edition published 2014 by Kingfisher
an imprint of Macmillan Children's Books
20 New Wharf Road, London N1 9RR
Associated companies throughout the world
www.panmacmillan.com

ISBN 978-0-7534-3750-6

Written by Dan Green
Consultant: Nick Chatterton
Designed and created by Basher www.basherbooks.com
Cover design: Jane Tassie

Dedicated to Emma Marbrook

9 8 7 6 5 4
4TR/0117/WKT/SCHOY(-)/128MA

A CIP catalogue record for this book
is available from the British Library.

Printed in China

Note to readers: the website addresses listed above are correct at
the time of going to print. However, due to the ever-changing nature
of the internet, website addresses and content can change. Websites
can contain links that are unsuitable for children. The publisher cannot
be held responsible for changes in website addresses or content, or for
information obtained through a third party. We strongly advise that
internet searches should be supervised by an adult.

CONTENTS

Introduction   4
Basic States   6
Nuts and Bolts   24
Nasty Boys   44
Lab Rats   54
'Orrible Organics   68
Bright Sparks   80
Earthy Resources   94
Chemicals for Life   106
Index   124
Glossary   126

Introduction
Chemistry / Antoine Lavoisier

Welcome to the wonderful, wild and sometimes wacky world of chemistry. Full of alchemy and mystery, it's the oldest of all the sciences. Chemistry is the study of the stuff the world is made from – the physical and chemical properties of matter – and how it behaves in chemical reactions. This is the field that has given humankind a hundred thousand new whizzo materials, not to mention an understanding of the inner workings of life itself.

Chemists may think they have all the solutions, but Antoine Laurent Lavoisier (1743–94) had more than most. He realized air was made of several parts and that a very important part of it is released by plants and is also combined with hydrogen to make water. He called this part oxygen. Another finding of his was simple, but fundamental to chemical reaction: what goes in (the reactants) always weighs the same as what comes out (the products). Sadly, he wasn't appreciated in his day and was beheaded in the French Revolution. It was his unpopular day job as a taxman that did it for this father of modern chemistry.

Antoine Lavoisier

Chapter 1
Basic States

Kicking things off are a straightforward, no-nonsense gang who take a back-to-basics approach. These are the things that you can see, touch, feel and hold – matter. There's the basic building block of matter itself, Element (he's the one that really "matters"), and the way it combines in Compound and Mixture. You'll find it in three forms: Solid, Liquid and Gas, the so-called "states of matter". The altogether more frisky Melting Point and Boiling Point, control when and how matter melts or boils and changes its character.

Solid

Liquid

Gas

Melting Point

Boiling Point

Brownian Motion

Element

Compound

Mixture

The Periodic Table

Solid
■ Basic States

☀ This stubborn old goat is the lowest-energy state of matter
☀ Chunky hunk whose particles have a rigid internal structure
☀ Heating makes its particles vibrate and melt into a liquid

Trustworthy and dependable, I don't go in for anything showy or high energy. I'm built properly and meant to keep my shape. With high melting points, I definitely don't flow. I'll sit motionless instead, which is handy if you want to make objects out of me, or use me to contain playful, slippery Liquid.

With my atoms closely packed, I resist squeezing and changing volume. My atoms often have a crystal structure – a regularly repeating pattern, but certain solids, such as glass, have an amorphous (random) internal structure. Raising my internal energy (for example, by heating) will eventually turn me to liquid. Polymers are solids with long, flexible molecules, making them plastic. Proteins are biological solids found in all living matter.

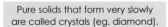

Pure solids that form very slowly are called crystals (eg. diamond).

● Densest: osmium (23 x heavier than water)
● Lightest: aerogel (530 x lighter than water)
● Lightest metal: lithium (floats on water)

Solid

Liquid
Basic States

- ✴ This fluid fellow flows through your arteries and veins
- ✴ A medium-energy state of matter that can't exist in a vacuum
- ✴ Heating turns this chap into a gas; freezing turns him into a solid

Nothing much bothers me, man. Like an old-school beatnik, I'm easygoing and I just go with the flow. If there are obstacles in my way I work around them and I change my shape to fit easily in any container you choose.

I'm an important fellow – without water on this planet, for example, life wouldn't be possible. But I am fussy about who I mix with. Sometimes I slip right in with other liquids, but other times I plain refuse. You can see this in the rainbow drops of oil in dirty puddles. Mutual attraction between my molecules causes surface tension, a force that makes me form drops. I resist being compressed and I expand when heated. If you heat me up or decrease the pressure around me, I'll eventually evaporate away as gas. When I dissolve a solid, I'm called a solvent.

Liquid mercury, with its high surface tension, is actually dry!

- ● Number of liquid elements: 2
- ● Liquid elements: Bromine, Mercury
- ● Amount of body weight that's water: 70 %

Liquid

Gas

Basic States

☀ This highest-energy state of matter has plenty of get up and go
☀ A chap of no fixed shape or volume, with energy to burn
☀ Measured in °C, and not greatly affected by pressure

I fizz, crackle and pop – I literally hum with energy. Freed from the tiresome bonds that bind Solid and Liquid, my particles dart about like hyperactive bees.

I'm tricksome and can disappear in front of your eyes, dispersing into thin air. Although I can be coloured, like green chlorine gas, I am usually invisible, like the air all around you. My unconfined nature means that I have no choice but to fill any container I am put in. Squeeze me into a can and my particles bash against the sides, exerting a force that is felt as pressure. Heating me up makes my particles move about faster and also has the effect of increasing the pressure. But squeeze me hard enough and you can calm my exuberance enough to turn me into a liquid. I can take the pressure, but can you?

Mustard gas is very poisonous and was first used as a weapon in WWI.

- Lightest gas: hydrogen
- Heaviest at 25°C: tungsten hexaflouride
- Heaviest element gas: radon

Gas

Melting Point

Basic States

- ☀ This sticky fellow is the point at which a solid turns to liquid
- ☀ A measure of how easily forces inside solids are broken
- ☀ Measured in °C, but not affected by pressure

I'm soft and schmaltzy and my crooning will melt Solid's heart. The forces between atoms and molecules in Solid are strong and stable, so it takes energy to break them. When you heat up a solid, its particles vibrate more and more until, finally, they have enough internal energy to break apart. Measure the temp as Solid turns to mush, and you have found me!

Melting Point

When a solid turns straight into a gas, this is called sublimation.

- ● Melting point of ice (sea level): 0 °C
- ● Highest m.p. (element): 3695 °C (tungsten)
- ● Lowest m.p. (element): −268.98 °C (helium)

Boiling Point
Basic States

* The point at which a liquid boils and turns to a gas
* A measure of how easily forces inside liquids are overcome
* Measured in °C, and very obviously affected by pressure

Boiling Point

I'm a fiery cauldron fizzing with rage. Roiling and bubbling, I vent my fury on Liquid. The molecules that make up Liquid are much less tightly bound to each other than they are in Solid, but they still have a definite tendency to bunch together. I teach 'em to stand on their own two feet, by busting apart their intermolecular forces and turning them into a gas!

● Boiling point of water (sea level): 100 °C
● Highest b.p. (element): 5560 °C (tungsten)
● Lowest b.p. (element): –268.98 °C (helium)

Water on top of Mount Everest boils at about 70 °C.

Brownian Motion

Basic States

- ☀ Stinky browny-pants who shows how tiny particles move about
- ☀ Makes molecules bash blindly about the place
- ☀ Thermal energy (heat) is the biggest mixer of molecules in liquids

For a chemistry thingumabob with such a sensible name, I am a very silly character. I say stuff like "nip skeep wibble wibble", because everything about me is random! You might not be able to tell what I'm going to do next, but you can easily predict my overall random behaviour.

I describe the way particles move about in liquid and gas. Seen under a microscope, a tiny pollen grain will jitter about in water as if it's alive – well, that's what Mr Brown first thought. Mr Einstein worked out that the "random walk" happens because the particle is being battered about by the invisible motion of molecules in the liquid. This explains how smells spread: by a process of diffusion, stinky molecules are jostled and dispersed until... phwoar, who dropped one?!

This theory is a big player in the microworld of nanotechnology.

- ● Named after: Robert Brown (1827)
- ● First recorded by: Jan Ingen-Housz (1785)
- ● First explained by: Albert Einstein (1905)

Brownian Motion

Element
Basic States

* A kind of goody two-shoes that makes up every substance
* Elementary character made of atoms all of the same kind
* One of the building blocks of matter, listed in the Periodic Table

Pure and simple, I am the basic stuff of everything you see in the Universe. With my 118 unique versions and almost no limit to the possible combinations I can make, there's already a mind-boggling number of compounds in existence and chemists make new ones by combining me in different proportions, or in novel ways.

Each of my versions is a unique variety made up of just one type of atom. My lightest variety is hydrogen, with a single proton in its nucleus. Next up is helium, with two protons and two neutrons. This pattern carries on all the way to the odd, unstable and very short-lived elements with a hundred or more protons (and attendant cargo of neutrons) in their central nuclei.

Most reactive metal is francium; most reactive non-metal is fluorine.

● No. naturally occuring elements: 92
● Most common: hydrogen
● Heaviest: element 118 (ununoctium)

Element

Compound

Basic States

☀ This chemical masterchef combines elements into new substances
☀ Produced and broken apart by Chemical Reaction
☀ Most substances on Earth are in the form of compounds

My creations are the perfect pudding – a combo of all the right elements in just the right proportions. Chemicals like to cosy up with each other and, with the help of ionic and covalent bonding, I allow them to do this in a way that benefits both elements. But once my ingredients have been fused together it's hard to separate them.

Compound

Oxygen is a compound of two oxygen atoms (O_2).

● Total no. of known compounds: 61 million
● Ionic compound: eg. salt
● Covalent compound: eg. water

Mixture
Basic States

- ☀ This mixed-up puppy is one smooth blender
- ☀ His recipes can be separated by physical means
- ☀ Chemical Reaction takes no part in this kind of combination

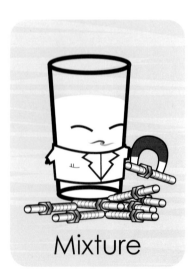

Mixture

I'm a real smoothie. I blend substances together – there's no sweat, none of Compound's heated reactions, just a relaxed merging of one substance with another. Like a bag of pick-and-mix sweets, I'm all mixed up, but each bit can still be separated by physical means (eg. with your sticky fingers!). Liquid mixtures need to be separated using special techniques like distillation.

- ● Solid mixtures: eg. concrete, soil
- ● Liquid mixtures (solution): eg. salt water
- ● Solid-liquid mixtures: eg. milk

Tap water is a mixture; distilled water is a pure substance.

The Periodic Table
Basic States

- An elegant way of organizing all known elements into a table
- Groups run vertically and periods run horizontally
- Invented by Siberian superchemist, Dimitri Mendeleev, in 1869

Hup-two! Hup-two! I'm a parade ground sergeant-major and it's my job to open a can of whup-ass for the elements. I whip these chemicals into shape. Yessirree!

A stickler for organization, I get all 118 elements to line up in groups, rows and blocks. Groups (vertical columns) of elements share similar properties. Periods (horizontal rows) each represent a new energy level filled up with electrons. The type of substance and its chemistry (reactivity) changes as you move down a group or move along a period, depending on whether an element is happier to lose or gain electrons from its outer shell. In fact, you can tell an element's personality by where it is in the table. Metals cluster on the left-hand side and non-metals on the right.

Element 101, Mendelevium, is named after Mendeleev.

- Group 1: reactive metals
- Elements in centre: transition metals
- Group 18: inert, or noble, gases

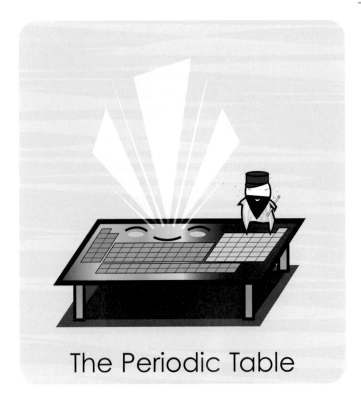

The Periodic Table

Chapter 2
Nuts and Bolts

Modest and unassuming, this bunch of founding fathers is rarely glimpsed. Yet these backroom movers and shakers are the parts that make up matter – the stuff from which the whole universe is made. Their properties govern the stately flow of energy as bonds uncouple and re-link, as atoms and molecules move from one compound to another. And it's their behind-the-scenes activities that underpin chemical reactions and give the Lab Rats all the bubble and explosion they need. You've got to keep your "Ion" this lot, they're nuts!

Atom

Isotopes

Ion

Simple Molecule

Giant Molecule

Polymer

Metallic Bonding

Nanoparticles

Avogadro's Number

Mole

Smart Materials

Atom
■ Nuts and Bolts

✴ Smaller than a pinprick, but larger than life
✴ Atomic particle that has no overall electrical charge
✴ The Periodic Table is arranged in atomic number order

I am the stuff the Universe is made of. I'm every chemical compound – in fact, I'm everything you can see, touch and breathe. I am like a planetary system in miniature. My central nucleus is made of tightly packed, positively-charged protons and neutral neutrons. Orbiting in energy levels (called shells) around this heavy, positive core are my zippy, negatively-charged electrons. The shells wrap around the nucleus like the layers of an onion, and are filled from the bottom up. The first shells hold two electrons, the second eight and the third 18.

I hold onto my protons and neutrons for dear life. The number of protons determines what kind of element I am, but it's the electrons in my outer shell that I use for chemistry, by pairing-and-sharing with other atoms, or shifting across to other atoms to create ions.

Half a million atoms could line up across a single human hair.

● Number of electrons = no. of protons
● Atomic number. = no. of protons
● Mass number = no. of protons + neutrons

Atom

Isotopes
■ Nuts and Bolts

✹ Atoms with equal atomic numbers, but different mass numbers
✹ Goblins with varying numbers of neutrons in their atomic nucleus
✹ Isotopes that decay (break apart) are called radioisotopes

Like the ghastly creations of some crazed professor in a duff sci-fi movie, we're Atom's monstrous brothers. With the same number of protons as our atomic sibling, we have the same chemistry and undergo the same reactions. However, we have a different number of neutrons in our nuclei – sometimes more, sometimes less.

This unhealthy amount of neutrons gives us a nasty streak. A normal atom is usually stable, but our unbalanced cores can lose protons and neutrons, or gain protons, in nuclear radiation – changing element type in the process! Medicine makes clever use of our radioactive decay, but we are famous for our destructive power: radon isotopes in granite give people cancer, while uranium-235 and plutonium-239 are the active ingredient in nuclear weapons.

Doctors use barium isotopes to trace the passage of food through the guts.

● Carbon-12 (6 protons, 6 neutrons) = ^{12}C
● Carbon-14 (6 protons, 8 neutrons) = ^{14}C
● $^{14}Carbon$: used in carbon dating

Isotopes

Ion
▪ Nuts and Bolts

☀ An atom that has gained or lost one or more electrons
☀ Strong electrostatic forces hold these chaps together
☀ Makes metals and non-metals join in "salty" crystal lattices

Let's get this party started! It's all well and good to admire Atom's steadiness, but you want a bit of spark and pizzazz in your chemistry set, don't you?

No atom, apart from the Group 8 elements, has a full set of electrons in its outer shell. My trick is to transfer electrons to or from the outer shells to fill them up. This creates positively and negatively charged ions, making lots of exciting chemical reactions possible – opposites attract! I join positive metal and negative non-metal ions together in a tight embrace with my ionic bonds. The "ionic compounds" are rock solid with high melting and boiling points; brittle crystals that dissolve in polar solvents (like water); and conductors of electricity when molten or in solution.

Table salt (sodium chloride) is a well-known ionic compound.

● Groups 1 & 2 (metals): lose electrons
● Groups 6 & 7 (non-metals): gain electrons
● Melting point of salt (NaCl): 801 °C

Ion

Simple Molecule
Nuts and Bolts

- Two or more atoms held together by a covalent bond
- Covalent bonding shares electrons between atoms
- This calm character often forms between non-metals

There's nothing flashy about me. I am a safe pair of hands who is more like a geography teacher in a faded old suit than a superhero. Quiet and unfussy, I let two or more non-metals combine, making electrically neutral, stable substances, such as water and nitrogen.

Rather than rob atoms of their electrons, transferring them about willy-nilly (like that reprobate Ion), I prefer to allow non-metal atoms to co-operate in filling their outer electron shells. This flexible and strong form of chemical bonding is called covalent bonding and is used by many simple molecules. My covalent compounds have low melting and boiling points because, although the bonds between atoms are strong, the forces of attraction between electrically neutral molecules are weak.

H_2O is a covalent compound of two hydrogen atoms and one oxygen atom.

- Bonds between atoms: very strong
- Intermolecular forces: very weak
- Smallest molecule: hydrogen (0.00000015 mm)

Simple Molecule

Giant Molecule

■ Nuts and Bolts

* This diamond geezer is a girl's best friend
* Whopper latticework with a huge number of bonds
* A titan who works best with carbon, silicon and oxygen

I'm a covalent colossus, a behemoth of bonding. Atoms in my mammoth molecules are linked by strong covalent bonds, like a towering superstructure of interlinked girders. As each atom is tightly bonded to its neighbours, I am usually very hard, sometimes brittle and have a very high melting point – and that's why diamonds are forever!

Giant
Molecule

Carbon forms diamond, graphite and insane spheres called buckyballs!

● Hardest mineral: diamond
● Melting/boiling point: very high
● Melting point of diamond: 3600 °C

Polymer

Nuts and Bolts ■

* Chains of small molecules form this "Mr Poly" giant molecule
* This multi-purpose chap comes in a thousand useful forms
* Man-made plastics are the wonder material of the last century

Polymer

I'm plastic, and I'm possible because millions of simple, repeating hydrocarbon molecules (monomers) can join up into giant, chain-link molecules. I have my naturally occurring varieties, but my man-made types, which are cheap to produce, can be anything you want them to be: pliable or rigid, soft or hard. For a groovy 70s vibe, just check out polyester – it's like one long daisy chain!

● Natural polymers: cellulose, amber
● Man-made polymers: nylon, PVC
● Reaction called: polymerization

Used to make plastic bags, bottles, wellies, clothes, surgical implants...

Metallic Bonding

■ Nuts and Bolts

- ☀ Behind-the-scenes character that binds Metal's atoms together
- ☀ A lattice of positive ions surrounded by a sea of free electrons
- ☀ A big softie, who is the reason why Metal is a good conductor

Inside the dark heart of that hardcase metalhead, Metal, you'll find me. One of three important types of chemical bonding, I link metal atoms, just like ionic bonding links ions and covalent bonding chemically joins molecules.

The properties of metals are all down to the way I bind their atoms. Internally, metals are arranged into networks of positive ions with "seas" of electrons washing around in between. Electrostatic forces of attraction between the ions and electrons hold the whole thing together, but the electrons are also free to move about through the giant structure. Because of this, metals are great conductors of heat and electricity. The flexible internal arrangement also allows metals to be shaped easily and hold an edge well. I'm one sharp cookie!

Metals are shiny because light hits the sea of electrons and is reflected.

- Best conductor: silver (1.59×10^{-8} Ωm)
- Hardest metal: tungsten carbide
- Melting point mercury: -38.83 °C

Metallic Bonding

Nanoparticles
■ Nuts and Bolts

* ☀ No blockheads, these titchy particles have unusual properties
* ☀ Nanoparticles behave very differently to larger lumps of stuff
* ☀ They get added to materials to lend them superpowers

We live in the realm of the itty-bitty. Forget the flea, things in our world are just a few atoms across. We are an array of dazzling shapes – cuboids, rods, spheres and bananas – that are all 10,000 times thinner than a cat's whisker.

With each of our minuscule particles come unexpected talents. Let's take a lump of regular silver. It has the natural properties to kill bacteria and fungi, whereas a sprinkling of nanosilver acts as a ruthless killer of germs and superbugs. Why? Because it has vastly more surface area to its volume, which makes the atoms at its surface much more reactive and powerful. Sometimes it is just our weeny size that makes us special: zinc oxide nanos – ace absorbers of UV light – are added to sunscreen because they're invisible to the naked eye.

Nanoparticles might have side effects on people and the environment.

* ● 1 nanometre = 0.000,000,001 m
* ● Size of nanoparticle: 1–10 nm
* ● Nanoscience is called nanotechnology

Nanoparticles

Avogadro's Number

■ Nuts and Bolts

☀ A real bigwig whose real name is Avogadro's constant
☀ A number that tells you how many molecules in a mole of gas

You can count on me, I'm a constant. My special number – like a dozen eggs – tells you exactly how many atoms you will find in a specific quantity of any gas at a certain pressure and temperature. This number is 6022 followed by 20 zeros. It's a very big number; if you had that many soft-drink cans, they would cover the planet in a blanket 322 km thick!

Avogadro's Number

Avogadro's constant:
6.022 141 79 (30) x 10^{23} mol^{-1}

● Named after: Amedio Avogadro
● 602,200,000,000,000,000,000,000 = no. of particles in one mole of substance

Mole

Nuts and Bolts ■

- This refined fellow isn't a mole who lives in a hole!
- A unit of measurement – or high-minded chemical counting!
- One mole (symbol: mol) has 6.02×10^{23} particles

Mole

Atoms are very small and fiendishly fiddly to count, so I help out with a clever bit of backward thinking. A one-mole serving of any element or compound always contains the same amount of atoms or molecules, as given by Avogadro's number. The weight of each mole is equal to the atomic mass of each element, measured in grams (eg. 1 mole of elemental oxygen = 16 g).

- Mass of 1 mole of substance = molar mass
- 1 mole = the number of particles in 12 g of pure carbon

A mole of gaseous oxygen (O_2) = 16 x 2 = 32 g

Smart Materials

* Futuristic new materials with whizzo properties
* Sensitive souls who respond to heat, electricity, pH and stress
* Sharp and intelligent… and out to change the world!

We're smart cookies! We point to a wild time ahead where materials will respond to changes in the external environment. But don't think there is anything pie-in-the-sky about us. One of our gang includes the clever voltage-sensitive (electrochromic) material in LCDs that changes the colour and transparency of the screen. That's sharp!

We can give metals and plastics a "memory" by sprinkling in some Nanoparticles. Our technology is used in some glasses frames: squash them and our shape memory alloy (SMA) will bend back to its original shape, without any help from you! We can even "learn" certain behaviour. One day your toilet seat will warm up when you sit on it, your wallpaper will play music when you enter a room and your fridge will change colour to suit your mood. Sweet!

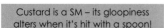

Custard is a SM – its gloopiness alters when it's hit with a spoon!

● First used: early 1980s
● Smart memory plastics called: SMPs
● Common SMA: nitinol (nickel-titanium alloy)

Smart Materials

Chapter 3

Nasty Boys

Quick! On with the safety goggles and gloves, the bad lads of chemistry are on the loose! This caustic lot are the original chemical nasties, causing chaos wherever (and on whoever) they land. Belligerent bullies they may be, but the ability of Acid and Base to take to Water and release reactive ions gets them involved in tons of reactions. Sure, they push their weight about, but don't underestimate their usefulness to chemists and industry. They have their minders too: pH is measured with Universal Indicator, which tells you how strong each bad lad is.

Acid

Base

pH

Universal Indicator

Acid
■ Nasty Boys

- ☀ A searing chemical nasty with a low pH
- ☀ Donor of positive H^+ ions, it's the chemical opposite of base
- ☀ Wear gloves when handling this sour old soul

The most notorious of the Nasty Boys, I'm mad, bad and thoroughly dangerous to know. Given half a chance, I'll eat through metals and burn through your skin!

What gives me my acidic nature is my ability to lose hydrogen ions. I'm a complete splitter: in the presence of water, I disassociate, breaking into a negative ion and a positive hydrogen ion (H^+). This little plus-fella is a spare proton (which is why I'm also called a proton donor). It's free to react with other chemicals in a solution and create ten types of havoc! Really strong acids instantly let loose 100 per cent of their H^+ ions, while weak acids disassociate much less. Strong sulfuric acid is number one in the chemicals industry; weak acetic acid is number one when sprinkled on your chips as vinegar.

Phosphoric acid eats rust and makes fizzy drinks lip-smackingly good!

- ● Strong but mild: carborane superacid
- ● Weak but corrosive: hydrogen fluoride
- ● Acid pH: numbers less than 7

Acid

Base
Nasty Boys

- A basic chemical bad guy with a high pH
- Donor of negative OH⁻ ions, it's the chemical opposite of acid
- Wear gloves when handling this caustic chap

I'm a lowdown, cheatin' gunslinger. Base by nature, Base by name – "Base" is the chemical way of saying that solutions containing me have a pH above 7. My most common types are called alkalis. These are hydroxides of alkali metals or alkaline earth metals (Groups 1 and 2 of The Periodic Table) that give basic solutions in Water. All alkalis are bases, but not all bases are alkalis. Ammonia – found in bleach – is a base but not an alkali.

Acids play fast and loose with their positive H^+ ions, but I hoard them. I love 'em so much that when mixed with Water I nick them from the H_2O molecules! This floods a solution with super-reactive OH⁻ ions (Water minus a hydrogen ion). Household cleaners with me on board wipe the floor… and then lick the toilet bowl clean!

Caustic soda has the frightening ability to melt fat and unblock drains!

- Strong base: sodium hydroxide
- Weak base: ammonia
- Basic pH: numbers more than 7

Base

pH

Nasty Boys

- ✹ Measure of a solution's acidity, or the amount of H^+ ions
- ✹ Relative scale: low values are acidic and high values are basic
- ✹ This "pHella" is crucial to body and ocean chemistry

I'm the "pHantom": a secret agent with the codename pH. That's right, you got it. Small p. Big H. I infiltrate solutions to probe them for acidic activity. I then assign a number, from 0 to 14, to every solution. The more H^+ ions drifting about, the more acidic they are and lower the number. Calm and unbiased, pH 7 is my magic number who sits in the neutral zone. Above this, solutions are proper basic!

"pHenomenally" important in your body's tricky chemical environment, my pH has to be just so for a staggering number of complex reactions to go off "pHlawlessly". When you exercise, your blood gets ever so slightly more acidic, from CO_2 released by cells breaking down carbohydrates and fat for energy – but too much acid in your blood causes a total shutdown of your body system!

The abbreviation pH stands for the "power of hydrogen".

- ● Blood pH: 7.4 (called "physiological pH")
- ● pH of pure, distilled water: 7
- ● pH of rainwater: about 5.2

pH

Universal Indicator

Nasty Boys

* Simple way of testing for pH
* Indicates pH values with a spectrum of colours
* This universal policeman is found on handy strips of paper

I'm the detective of the Nasty Boys. With such a dangerous group, it's nice to know you have a friendly bobby like me padding about nearby. When faced with an unknown solution, I let you know how acidic or basic it is. I inform you what you're up against with a simple change of colour.

I indicate the entire range of the pH scale: the values from 0 to 14. Actually, I am a cunning mixture of different substances that change colour at different values. I'm found in books of tear-off strips, which can be dipped into mystery solutions to tell you their acidity. I'm also found in liquid form. My individual components can be used in chemistry tests, called titrations, which tell you the precise end point of a chemical reaction with a "blush" of colour. This is one way to find the concentration and purity of a solution.

The pigment in red cabbage juice is a natural universal indicator.

● Red: indicates strong acid
● Green: indicates neutral
● Purple: indicates strong base

Universal Indicator

Chapter 4
Lab Rats

Bubble, bubble, toil and trouble! This troop of mad-cap mavericks provide a playing field for some of science's most dangerous experiments. Their crazy shapes and twisted spirals of glass are a real "smash" and the stock-in-trade of anyone intent on chemical capers, from the early alchemists who tried to turn lead into gold, to the modern-day biochemist separating DNA on a gel, or the inorganic chemist refluxing a super-duper new catalyst. Master the use of this equipment and you'll go a long way in chemistry – just remember, never lick the spoon!

Bunsen Burner

Thermometer

Test Tube

Pipette

Filter

Distillation

Precipitate

Chromatography

Bunsen Burner
■ Lab Rats

☀ Life's a natural gas for this burner who does hot work in the lab
☀ A "hole"-hearted fellow who heats, sterilizes and combusts
☀ This flaming beauty burns between 750 °C and 950 °C

The undisputed king of the Lab Rats, I burn like a beacon, taking centre stage in a theatre of bangs, bubblings and strange whiffs. I'm used for flame tests (to identify what type of metal is in a compound) and for heating stuff up.

The cunning part of Mr Bunsen's invention is an air hole at my base, near the gas inlet. With the hole fully open the air-gas mixture is at its richest, allowing complete combustion and a roaring-hot flame. Watch out! On this setting the flame burns a nearly invisible blue, with two very distinct cones – the hottest part is the inner cone. When you just need me to tick over, switch to my cool, orange-yellow safety flame. Closing the hole allows the gas to mix with air only at the head of my chimney, which results in incomplete combustion and a safer, cooler flame!

Soot in the safety flame reflects light and makes it burn luminous yellow.

● Invented by: Robert Bunsen (1854)
● Built by: Peter Desdega (lab assistant)
● Fuel: natural gas (methane)

Bunsen Burner

Thermometer

■ Lab Rats

※ A hothead who measures temperature in °C and °F
※ Uses mercury or alcohol, which rises up the stem
※ The stem is a very thin hollow tube of glass

I'm a little piece of magic you can hold in your hand – a true chemical wizard. Heat is a very strange concept to pin down. It's something you can only feel. Until a liquid boils, for example, it's very hard to see how hot or cold it is. Yet I turn that reality on its head and allow you to "see" temperature and read it off a calibrated (fixed) scale.

You have to handle me with care. I'm a delicate soul in a slender package. Surrounded by glass, my central column is a vacuum, which makes my liquid independent of Air's pressure. I work on the basis that materials expand and contract as they get hotter and colder. The longer my line, the higher the temperature reading. I am calibrated against known temperatures, such as the freezing and the boiling point of water, to make sure I'm accurate.

From the Greek words for "heat" (therme) and "measure" (metron).

● Celsius scale invented by: A Celsius (1742)
● Mercury scale range: –38 °C to 357 °C
● Alcohol scale range: –114 °C to 78 °C

Thermometer

Test Tube

■ Lab Rats

✳ A chemical lovely used to mix and store substances
✳ Made of special glass that doesn't expand when heated
✳ Sometimes has a stopper, or bung, to shut it up

Hold me, shake me, mix me and heat me up! I'm the pin-up of the lab. Made of glass, I'm slim, tall and curved of lip, with a round bottom. I'm the playground on which most of chemistry – organic and inorganic – is played out. Finger-size, I usually lounge about in test-tube racks, or am held tightly in the grip of a test-tube holder. Oh, I do love to cause a reaction!

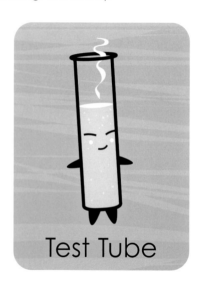

Test Tube

An oxide of boron makes test-tube glass heat resistant.

● Made of: Pyrex glass
● Length: 50 mm to 200 mm
● Width: 10 mm to 20 mm

- A cheeky little squirt used to transfer specific amounts of liquid
- This chemical dropper is made of glass and rubber
- Delivers a smashingly accurate volume

Pipette

I'm a chemist's best friend. My simplest form looks like an eye dropper with a squeezy rubber bulb. You will find loads of different types of me in the lab, but my basic job is always the same: I suck up liquid from one container and deliver it to another as scampish squirts or drops. My most whizzy model is the piston-driven micropipette, which delivers tiny amounts with great accuracy.

- Smallest: zeptoliter pipette
- Used with a burette for titration
- Micropipette invented by: W Gilson (1972)

Biochemists and forensic scientists use micropipettes.

Filter
■ Lab Rats

* A one-way door that only allows liquids or gases through
* Winkles out solids that have got mixed with liquids or gases
* Firefighters rely on filters to breathe in smoke-filled buildings

I'm a canny operator who can get you out of a fix. Got Solid mixed up with Liquid? I make quick work of separating them. With the aid of a filter funnel and a cone of filter paper, I create a barrier that lets Liquid through, but blocks Solid. No job is too small. You'll even find me making your coffee – well, filtering out the coffee grounds before you drink it.

Filter

Filters "scrub" the air entering skyscrapers to remove smog particles.

● Liquid filtered called: filtrate
● Solid left on paper called: residue
● Other uses: teabags, fuel filters

Distillation

Lab Rats

- ☀ This "moonshiner" is a method of separating and purifying liquids
- ☀ Rascalish bubbler and boiler who separates crude oil into fractions
- ☀ Essential operator for the oil, plastics and chemicals industries

Distillation

I'm a bootlegger and old-school scoundrel. My technique purifies and separates two or more liquids. Every liquid has a slightly different boiling point, so heating up a mixture of liquids brings each one to the boil at a different temperature. In this way, I drive off the substance with the lowest boiling point first and collect it in a separate vessel.

- ● Earliest known use: 500BCE
- ● Fractional distillation separates crude oil into: bitumen, diesel, jet fuel, petroleum

Used to make alcoholic drinks, such as whisky, purer and more potent.

Precipitate

■ Lab Rats

☀ Stand-offish solid formed in a solution during a chemical reaction
☀ Lets impurities be removed, or solids produced, from solutions
☀ Used for making paint pigments and water safe to drink

Hanging like a gloomy cloud in a chemical mixture, I occur when an insoluble compound forms in a liquid mixture. Because of my unfriendly talents and refusal to mix-in-and-make-do, I am used to separate things out of liquids. Solids that don't dissolve in liquids are very handy as they will fall to the bottom of the liquid under gravity and settle on their own. Or they can be filtered out or even spun out of the solution in a centrifuge – now, that's a dizzying option!

I'm often mucky and nondescript, but sometimes I appear in the garish hues that any dayglo-wearing clubber would die for! In this guise, I am used in paint pigments. Potassium iodide added to lead nitrate, for example, results in a beautiful precipitate of bright yellow lead iodide. Yeowch!

Precipitation is used to remove the impurities from drinking water.

● Process called: precipitation
● Solid formed called: precipitate
● Liquid remaining called: supernate

Precipitate

Chromatography
■ Lab Rats

- ☀ Colourful crime investigator used by forensic scientists
- ☀ Separates the contents of complex mixtures for analysis
- ☀ Parts of a mixture move at different speeds, which separates them

Anyone in need of a little TLC? Slide over here, I'm your main squeeze! Although chemists might need some Tender Loving Care every now and again, they're more likely to be happier with Thin-Layer Chromatography – ha, ha! Joking aside, I'm a fully paid-up Lab Rat. My analytical skills are used to make DNA fingerprints and this exciting crime-stopping streak brings some colour to the lab!

I'm used to separate mixtures in a solution. Try me out for yourself. Just make a dot with a marker pen close to the bottom of a strip of filter paper; dip the end into a shallow dish of water and leave overnight. As the water seeps up the paper column, the components in the ink mixture separate themselves out at different rates. This is exactly how CSI chaps analyze dye found at a crime scene.

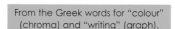

From the Greek words for "colour" (chroma) and "writing" (graph).

- ● Sample for analysis called: extract
- ● Types: paper, gas, liquid, "tlc"
- ● World's smallest column: 1 mm (2010)

Chromatography

Chapter 5
'Orrible Organics

Once upon a time, this group of compounds were thought to be made only by living organisms, so they were given the name "organic". But then some busybody chemist managed to make the sticky yellow substance urea (which occurs naturally in urine) in a lab, using potassium cyanate and ammonium sulphate salts. Hmmm, nothing "organic" there. But the name was a good 'un, so it stuck. It now means the study of compounds of carbon – the basis of life on Earth. Hydrocarbons form the backbone of this chemical clan and of most organic compounds.

Hydrocarbons

Alcohol

Carboxylic Acids

Esters

Dyestuffs

Hydrocarbons
'Orrible Organics

- Slick molecules with skeletons made of hydrogen and carbon
- Almost all smarmy Hydrocarbons are derived from crude oil
- They are "cracked" (split) to produce new and useful chemicals

Howdy doody! We're the quick, slick oilman – a big-bucks Texas sugar daddy! Our smorgasbord of combustible compounds, produced by fractional distillation of crude oil, supplies much of the world's fuel. Don't think we're only good for fuel though. We're cracked to produce a bunch of valuable chemicals, whom you're about to meet!

Our simplest version, called methane, has just one carbon atom with four covalently bonded hydrogen atoms – you release it when you fart. Simple Hydrocarbons like this are gases, but the melting and boiling points increase as the number of carbons in the chain increases. With five or six carbon atoms, we are liquids at room temperature; with increasing numbers you'll find us as waxes, low-melting solids and solid polymers.

Lakes of liquid methane and ethane have been found on Titan.

- Formula of methane: CH_4
- First oil well drilled: Baku, Azerbaijan (1948)
- Largest oil reserves: Middle East (63 % of total)

Hydrocarbons

Alcohol

'Orrible Organics

- ☀ Liquid party animal who makes things go with a pop
- ☀ There are thousands of alcohols, including ethanol
- ☀ Ethanol is the colourless and volatile liquid in alcoholic drinks

I am very appealing and many folk find me intoxicating company. But be careful, because I can bite hard. As ethanol – the active ingredient in alcoholic drinks, I am the world's most notorious depressant. Scratch my glitzy surface and you find a drab, sad existence.

As a group of chemicals, however, I'm so much more than just ethanol. Glycol stays gloopy at very low temperatures, which makes it a handy antifreeze. My molecules are nothing more complicated than a hydrocarbon with an attached OH^- group. My OH^- group makes me "polar", with one slightly negatively charged and one slightly positively charged end. I'm also a super solvent for dissolving other polar compounds.

Yeast ferments sugar in ripe fruit to produce alcohol.

- ● Chemical formula ends in OH
- ● Formula of ethanol: C_2H_5OH
- ● Freezing point of ethanol: −114.3 °C

Alcohol

Carboxylic Acids
'Orrible Organics

* Mostly natural, weak acids that are soluble in water
* Smelly compounds that can be made from alcohols or esters
* Reacts with alcohols to make esters

You can spot most of us a mile off, 'cos our names all end in "oic". Methanoic acid (also called formic acid), for example, is a methane-based Carboxylic Acid. We're no "oiks" though – on the contrary, we're mild-mannered chemicals.

The Carboxylic Acids gang are brown-patches-on-the-elbows organic foodies, found in many natural products, such as: coconut oil (lauric acid), milk (lactic acid) and vinegar (acetic acid). As salicylic acid we provide pain relief in the form of aspirin, as well as treatments for warts and verrucas. We become more solid and waxy the longer our chains of carbon get – Carboxylic Acids with more than about ten atoms of carbon are called fatty acids, many of which are essential in the body.

Formic acid is the active ingredient in ant bites – and it stings!

● Chemical formula ends in COOH
● Formula of methanoic acid: HCOOH
● Odour: strong (eg. acetic acid in vinegar)

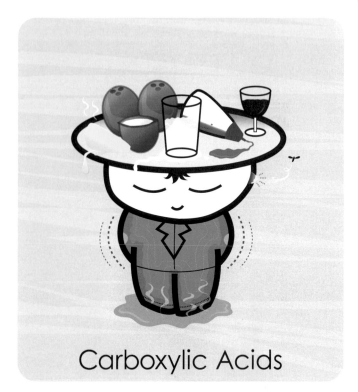

Carboxylic Acids

Esters

'Orrible Organics

☀ Fragrant food flavourings that are insoluble in water
☀ Found in perfumes, bodily hormones, plus fruits and berries
☀ Made from carboxylic acid and alcohol; smell of nail varnish

We're one fruity fancy! Wreathed in the fragrant fug of a flowery bouquet, our molecules can be all the flavours and colours of a smelly eraser collection: strawberry, cherry, lavender… you name it. When fresh, we give taste and smell to many natural fruits and berries; when fake, we're the main ingredient for artificial food flavourings. Just suck a pear drop. That acidic "fruit flavour" is us!

We're made in the pretty-sounding esterification reaction, when a carboxylic acid reacts with an alcohol (to make the peary smell in pear drops, pentanol is added to ethanoic acid). You can whiff us in the air, because we're more volatile than Carboxylic Acids and prone to evaporation. At full strength, we're found in industrial solvents. We're more than just a fake flavour!

They are well known as long polymers in polyesters.

● Chemical formula ends in COOR
● Most sweet: ethylethanoate (pear drops)
● Melting point (methyl methanoate): −100 °C

Esters

Dyestuffs
'Orrible Organics

- ☀ This fashionista's origins are lost in the mists of time
- ☀ Early dyes were made from plants and rusty earth pigments
- ☀ Embeds itself deep within the material – it's not like paint

Clothing the world in swirls of colours to "dye" for, I'm a total trendsetter. I give verve and va-va-voom to all sorts of materials, from acrylic threads in fluoro socks to bright paper, as well as imparting a sober dash to shoe leather!

Dyeing goes a lot deeper than just bathing something in coloured liquid. My chemical compounds are actually attracted to the substrate material, and sometimes need something called a mordant to fix the dye. Whereas Precipitate's insoluble colours just sit on top of the material, most of us become bonded to the fibre. I have thousands of different types. Your denims are stained in indigo – a vat dye, which needs a large keg of nasty alkaline liquor. The world's best-selling dye is Sulfur Black 1, which dyes – you guessed it – your socks!

WH Perkin made the first synthetic dye, mauve, in 1856.

- ● Earliest recorded use: China, 2600BCE
- ● Most expensive: lapis lazuli
- ● Vegetable dyes: beetroot, saffron

Dyestuffs

Chapter 6
Bright Sparks

This next group of chemical heartbreakers are the life and soul of chemistry. Everything you ever associated with this strange science – weird concoctions, fizzing explosions and seven kinds of chemical chaos – you'll find in this energetic bunch. It's enough to make you cackle like a mad scientist! The patron saint of all chemists – Chemical Reaction – provides most lab-coat wearers with a job; discovering its secrets and ways to make it work for the good of humankind is a lifetime's study. Now, sit back and let things go with a BANG!

Chemical
Reaction

Reactivity
Series

Combustion

Activation
Energy

Firework

Catalyst

Enzymes

Chemical Reaction

Bright Sparks

☀ A feisty fellow who mixes things up to produce visible changes
☀ Rates of reaction depend on concentration, pressure and temp
☀ A chemist's main tool, its workings are essential to industry

I'm gunning to get a reaction. I'm what chemistry is all about. When compounds bump into each other, chemical bonds get broken, and atoms, ions and molecules make new alliances. You can tell if I'm around – compounds change colour, thermometers go bonkers and precipitates appear out of nowhere... In short, my process is a chemical change where a substance is transformed into another.

I combine ingredients like a master baker. Sometimes there is no going back to the substances you started with – as with cake-baking. I either suck up energy in endothermic reactions, or give out energy in exothermic reactions. Chemists who know their reactions can zip about from one product to another, to synthesize the one they need.

The human body has 400 billion chemical reactions per second!

● Speed called: rate of reaction
● Ingredients called: reactants
● Results called: products

Chemical Reaction

Reactivity Series
Bright Sparks

* This safecracker tells you how violently a metal will react
* Key in reactions of metals with acids and displacement reactions
* Tells you how best to extract the metallic loot from ore

I'm an explosive idea and the secret behind some of the most spectacular reactions! I have a chart that tells you who will win in a head-to-head chemical competition.

I am a blueprint for the reactions of Metal. The more reactive the metal, the more readily it will lose electrons to form positive ions. Metals high up on my series are also stronger reducing agents, combining with oxygen to tarnish their shiny surfaces. Wanna know the secret? The number one reactive metal is potassium (steer clear), then sodium (you've been warned), lithium, calcium, magnesium, aluminium, zinc, iron, tin, lead, copper, silver, gold and, lastly, easy-going platinum. Now, wanna see something that will blow your lid? Check out a video of a 3000 °C thermite reaction.

Thermite: iron oxide + aluminium → molten iron + aluminium oxide.

* Fastest reactant: potassium
* Most reactive: potassium
* Least reactive: platinum

Reactivity Series

Combustion
Bright Sparks

☀ This sparky chap is an unholy burning terror
☀ Fuel and oxidant react to release heat and light
☀ A redox (or reduction–oxidation) reaction

Come closer. I'll warm you up, buddy. BOOM! I'll also leave you with a blackened face. I'm a law unto myself – I can be your friend on a cold night, or a flaming nuisance.

I am a highly specialized type of chemical reaction that occurs when a fuel combines completely with the oxygen component of air. This is most definitely an exothermic reaction, which is just a complicated word for "gives off heat". I've got energy to burn. As well as my more obvious dangers, my burning generates oxidized products, which are often pretty nasty. For example, fossil fuels burn to produce toxic carbon monoxide, lots of carbon dioxide, plus the acid-rain maker, sulfur dioxide. And when my oxidation reaction is incomplete, I leave minute particles of black carbon soot to waft skywards on my flame.

Materials with low ignition points are prone to spontaneous combustion.

● Combustion = chemical name for burning
● Point substance burns: ignition point
● Incomplete combustion: yellow flame

Combustion

Activation Energy

Bright Sparks

☀ A bright spark who kick-starts a chemical reaction
☀ The higher the AE, the more energy needed to start a reaction

Every chemical reaction needs some oomph to get it going. I am that minimum energy required. If you've ever seen a novice trying to light a fire, angry and covered in soot, you'll know that, unlike $H_2 + O_2$, coal needs more than a spark to combust. But it's not only Combustion who needs my kick. Before many compounds will react, stable chemical bonds must be broken.

Activation Energy

Rusting is a slow reaction, but with low AE since it occurs at room temperature.

● Sources of AE: heat, light
● AE needed to start reaction: energy barrier
● Reaction with low AE: spontaneous

Firework
Bright Sparks

- A showman with a joyful, impressive exothermic nature
- This dangerous dude's prime component is gunpowder
- Invented in China to scare away evil spirits

Firework

Exothermic or what! I'm a colourful show-off pyrotechnician with an explosive personality. I'm a punch packed into a paper tube – an extremely fast chemical reaction. My aim is to live fast and burn bright. Groups 1, 2 and transition metals are mixed with gunpowder (a fiery blend of potassium nitrate, charcoal and sulfur) to give me my explosion of peacock colours.

- First known use: 12th century
- Largest firework shell: 422 kg (Japan)
- Largest display: 500,000 fireworks (Dubai)

Barium compounds burn green;
magnesium compounds burn white.

Catalyst
Bright Sparks

* Makes reactions go faster, but doesn't affect their yield
* Decreases a reaction's activation energy
* This cool cat is not destroyed or changed during a reaction

Chemical engineers love me, 'cos I smooth the path for reactions, allowing them to proceed more easily. Despite all the hot stuff going on, I keep my cool and don't get used up in the course of the chemical jiggery-pokery.

I help produce most industrially important chemicals – you name it, I catalyse it! My "cat-alogue" of jobs includes refining petroleum, breaking down chains of Hydrocarbons (called catalytic cracking) and producing ammonia in the Haber process. I often allow intermediate compounds to form, providing a new pathway for a reaction to follow with a lower activation energy. Since less energy is used to start a reaction, it can happen at lower temperatures and faster too. I can also work by providing a larger surface area upon which a reaction can take place.

CFCs (chlorofluorocarbons) catalyse the breakdown of ozone.

* Top catalysts: zeolites, graphite, platinum
* Most common catalyst: H^+ (proton)
* Unit of catalytic activity: kat

Catalyst

Enzymes
Bright Sparks

✴ Catalysts for chemical processes in living things
✴ They make bodily reactions go a million times faster
✴ These swampy creatures are nearly always proteins

We're enzymes and we live in slime! We drip from your saliva, swim in your soupy stomach juices and slop in your cells. Our job is to chivvy along chemical reactions that break down your food, copy your DNA, transmit signals from your nerves and brain, and govern your emotions. We're no ordinary catalysts, since we're extremely picky about which individual reactions we assist. Which kind of us a cell stocks determines its metabolic function.

Our protein-gobbling powers also make us powerful commercial chemicals. You will find us breaking down fatty stains in biological washing powder, tenderizing meat and cleaning contact lenses. Our most accurate types are the restriction enzymes at the business end of copying and reproducing your DNA.

Drugs and poisons mess with the normal functioning of enzymes.

● Most common on Earth: RuBisCO
● Number in the body: about 4000
● Names of enzymes end in "-ase"

Enzymes

Chapter 7
Earthy Resources

Our planet is bursting with chemical surprises, but this resourceful team will keep you grounded. The air, sea and earth ultimately provide the raw material for all our planet's chemical shenanigans. From the year dot, these old-timers have satisfied dabblers' curiosity with materials and substances. This gang are often found combined in stable compounds and it can be hard to separate them. By studying the gang's structure and properties, and ways to purify them, chemists have been able to synthesize a staggering array of new materials and compounds.

Air

Seawater

Rock

Metal

Alloy

Fossil Fuels

Air

Earthy Resources

☀ An airhead who surrounds the planet
☀ This wet blanket can hold a great deal of water vapour
☀ At 100 km from Earth's crust, the Kármán line marks its upper limit

Airy fairy? Think again. I have you surrounded on all sides and you don't stand a chance of surviving without me, buster! I'm a collection of gases held loosely in place by Earth's gravity. My thin layer, called the atmosphere, wraps around the planet like a cosy blanket. Thanks to my mix of Greenhouse Gases, this heat sink evens out extremes of temperature between night and day and, with the help of Ozone, protects living things from the Sun's radiation.

I'm currently dressed mainly in Nitrogen and Oxygen, but until 2.5 billion years ago I was principally CO_2, along with choking volcanic nasties, such as ammonia and methane. As soon as photosynthesizing organisms evolved, they began consuming CO_2 and filling the atmosphere with lovely Oxygen – it was a breath of fresh air I can tell you!

The megatonnes of dust, pollen and pollutants don't count as air.

● Nitrogen in air: 78.08 %
● Oxygen in air: 20.95 %
● Carbon dioxide in air: 0.039 %

Air

Seawater
Earthy Resources

- A salty seadog who keeps the temperature of the Earth steady
- Its salts are washed out of continental rocks by rain and rivers
- It's evaporated to produce sea salt (mainly sodium chloride)

Avast ye landlubbers! You may call your precious planet Earth, but you know it belongs to me! I cover more than two-thirds of the world's surface and hold 97 per cent of its water in my oceans. Underestimate me at your peril!

As a swashbuckling rogue, I'm certainly worth my salt. You see, every kilogram of Seawater has about 35 grams of dissolved salts. While a desert rat might survive drinking me, any thirsty sailor found quaffing mo won't be so lucky – fatal concentrations of salt in the blood cause fits, seizures and a grisly death. My salt content makes me quite different to fresh water. Things float more readily due to my increased density, which makes it easier to swim in my waters. I also freeze at –2 °C, not 0 °C, which is why I rarely freeze over. "Sea" for yourself!

A mouthful contains millions of bacteria and thousands of plankton.

- Common salt: NaCl (sodium chloride)
- Salinity of seawater: 3.1 to 3.8 %
- Saltiest closed sea: Dead Sea

Seawater

Rock

Earthy Resources

* A solid, dependable character that makes up Earth's crust
* Made of stuck-together mineral grains (chemical compounds)
* Ores are rocks that contain minerals, gemstones or metals

I'm totally ore-some! I'm the stuff that forms like a crusty scab on the surface of Earth. You can thank me for keeping your feet on solid ground. Look closely and you'll see that all types of me are made of little grains.

When I'm made of interlocking mineral grains, cooled from molten rock, I'm called igneous; with more rounded grains I'm called sedimentary. Metamorphic rocks occur when pressure and heat in Earth's crust have altered my minerals. Rocks on the surface are slowly eroded by Water, wind and weather. Igneous rocks tend to be harder and less porous, but even they get ground down. Rivers and glaciers transport grains of minerals from old rocks to make new sedimentary rocks. It's a cycle that truly "rocks".

Metals and fossil fuels are found buried in rocks, like buried treasure.

* Aluminium ore: bauxite (Al_2O_3)
* Copper ore: chalcopyrite ($CuFeS_2$)
* Mercury ore: cinnabar (HgS)

Rock

Metal

Earthy Resources

* This co-operative fella is found in rock ore – and sure is useful
* Metallic bonds account for its bendability and conductivity
* Most metals corrode in the air by combining with oxygen

I'm your easily persuaded, pliable friend and a great conductor of heat and electricity. Base metals are my reactive lot who corrode easily and are found tightly bound to their ores. Ferrous metals are mainly magnetic, while noble metals are unreactive. The transition metals bring colour to Dyestuffs, Precipitate and Firework, and many are catalysts without equal.

Metal

An oxidized layer on the surface of metals stops them sticking together.

● Base metals: copper, lead, zinc, tin
● Ferrous metals: cast iron, pig iron, steel
● Noble metals: gold, silver, platinum

Alloy

Earthy Resources

* Man-made metals who put a bit of "steel" into Metal softies
* Often made by melting two metals to form a solid solution
* Alloys have a melting range instead of a melting point

Alloy

The Man of Steel, I give a backbone to spineless metals. I make them fit for purpose with properties that better suit their uses. Without me, "supermetal" would be, well, just plain old Metal. I add carbon to iron to make super-strong steel; tin to copper to make super-smooth bronze; copper to zinc to make cheapskate brass; and nickel to tin to make shape-memory nitinol.

● Carbon content of steel: 0.02 to 2.14 %
● Uses for steel: skyscrapers, bridges
● Uses for copper: bearings, statues

Muscle wire is a super-duper, shape-memory alloy.

Fossil Fuels
Earthy Resources

* A powerhouse trio who began life in ancient tropical swamps
* Full of energy, they are extracted by mining, oil wells and gas rigs
* Carbon compounds buried in the absence of oxygen

As untapped deposits of potential energy, we lie in the dark, secret depths of Earth as vast stores of carbon. When our three types of deposits (oil, coal and natural gas) react with oxygen in a combustion reaction, you get energy. If the name conjures up images of crumbly old crones, think again. We're formed from the mixed-up remnants of plants and animals that died millions of years ago.

Oil is squeezed out of these deposits or from fossilized beds of shellfish. It is often found above coal in the Earth. Thick crude oil is made of many hydrocarbons, which are separated out by fractional distillation into light, volatile fuels and gloopy, less flammable polymers. Natural gas is a much livelier customer and the cream of the crop. Our trio provides heat and electrical energy for the entire world.

Fuelled the 19th century Industrial Revolution and changed the world.

* Age: up to 650 million years
* Coal mined each year: 4 billion tonnes
* Burning releases CO_2 and sulfur dioxide

Fossil Fuels

Chapter 8
Chemicals for Life

Life is you, animals, plants – all living things. Life, like all things, uses chemicals and chemical compounds. Many of these are very adaptable, able to turn their hand to the hundreds of functions and chemical reactions that keep life ticking over. Among them, the same elements crop up again and again, in particular carbon, hydrogen, oxygen and nitrogen. Some, such as oxygen, have mainly been created by life for life. The most amazing is DNA, the miracle molecule capable of replicating itself and building new copies of animals and plants.

Water

Oxygen

Carbon Dioxide

Ozone

Greenhouse Gases

Chlorophyll

Protein

DNA

Carbon

Nitrogen

Water

Chemicals for Life

- ☀ Liquid mover and shaker who covers most of Earth's surface
- ☀ This wet and wild character is essential for life
- ☀ A universal solvent that can dissolve many other chemicals

I am the most famous chemical on Earth – everyone knows my formula, H_2O. Although I'm tasteless, colourless, odourless and neutral in terms of pH, I'm not a sit-on-the-fence kind of character. I run in rivers, shaping the land, and collect in the oceans. I hang out as water vapour in rainclouds. I sit frozen solid as polar ice caps.

Most biological processes depend on me. If I'm not present in the correct amounts in your body's cells, the chemical reactions won't go off properly. Because it takes a lot of energy to make me change state, I soak up temperature changes, protecting the planet from extremes of heat and cold. I transmit light – my transparent nature allows plants to be submerged and, because of this food supply, animals can live underwater, too.

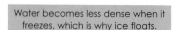

Water becomes less dense when it freezes, which is why ice floats.

- ● Earth's surface covered by water: 71 %
- ● Volume of water on Earth: 1.4 billion km³
- ● Per cent of water in human body: 55–78 %

Water

Oxygen

Chemicals for Life

- ☀ This non-metal is the component of air we breathe to survive
- ☀ The second most abundant element on Earth
- ☀ Its covalent bond splits to form oxides with other substances

Oi! I'm out to get a reaction. There's hardly an element on The Periodic Table I won't react with! I'd pick a fight in solitary confinement! I'm the most common element on Earth's surface, included in most compounds on air, sea and land. But it's as my colourless, odourless gas that I'm best known, because without me, you die!

I'm great at dissolving. I slip out of the air in your lungs into your bloodstream, then get transported to every cell in the body, where I power the burning of carbohydrates (sugars and starches) and fats for energy. I also dissolve in water, which is how fish and other watery animals survive. Cold water can hold more of me than warm, which is why the planet's polar waters have more abundant sealife. I am made industrially by fractional distillation of liquified air.

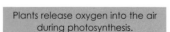

Plants release oxygen into the air during photosynthesis.

- ● Chemical formula: O_2
- ● Percentage of O_2 in air: 21%
- ● Discovered by: Joseph Priestley (1774)

Oxygen

Carbon Dioxide

■ Chemicals for Life

- ☀ This fizzy fellow is a major part of the carbon cycle
- ☀ Photosynthesis removes CO_2 from the air and releases O_2
- ☀ CO_2 is released naturally by volcanoes and geysers

I'm a bubbly character, brimming over with good cheer. You find me as the colourless, odourless gas used in soft drinks to give them a bit of fizz. I am meat and cheese for plantlife, who extract me from the air during photosynthesis. While plants are gulping down vast amounts of me, the animal world is breathing me out.

Be careful – I can go straight to your head. One per cent by volume of me in the air causes drowsiness – you've probably felt this in a hot, stuffy hall. Since my freezing point is relatively high, I can be stored solid as dry ice, which allows me to perform a smoky turn in stageshows. I'm also used to fight electrical fires. The oceans hoover me up, but in the atmosphere I'm a greenhouse gas, causing Earth to get hot under the collar.

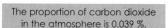

The proportion of carbon dioxide in the atmosphere is 0.039 %.

- ● Chemical formula: CO_2
- ● Freezing point: –78 °C
- ● Goes straight from a solid to a gas (sublimes)

Carbon Dioxide

Ozone

■ Chemicals for Life

☀ A light blue gas, dark blue when liquid, violet black when solid
☀ Pollutes at low levels and shields the Earth at high altitudes
☀ An allotrope of oxygen but less stable – better steer clear!

I'm a two-faced chemical. In polluted areas I form an irritating, throat-tickling smog. But I come into my own in the upper atmosphere. A thin layer of me, 10 to 50 km up, is enough to protect Earth from the worst of the Sun's ultraviolet rays. Trouble is, man-made chlorofluorocarbon molecules (CFCs) knock a hole in this layer over the South Pole every year.

Ozone

The largest ozone hole ever was 29.5 million km2 (Sept. 2006).

● Chemical formula: O_3
● Melting point: −192.5 °C
● Boiling point: −111.9 °C

Greenhouse Gases

Chemicals for Life ■

- Bad lad GGs who horse around in the Earth's atmosphere
- They absorb and reflect infrared radiation back to Earth
- Have been on the up since the start of the Industrial Revolution

Greenhouse Gases

Thanks to our ability to absorb radiation, we keep Earth toasty and life ticking over. Problems start with heat soaked up by the surface and radiated back. Instead of letting it shoot off into space, we absorb it and beam it back to Earth, which gets hotter. Our numbers are boosted by human activities, such as burning fossil fuels and chopping down forests.

- Warming effect = greenhouse effect
- Effect due to water vapour: 36–70 %
- Effect due to CO_2: 9–26 %

Main GGs are water vapour, CO_2, methane, nitrous oxide and ozone.

Chlorophyll
■ Chemicals for Life

- ☀ This miracle molecule has mastered the trick of photosynthesis
- ☀ Puts the green in greenery and allows plants to feed and grow
- ☀ Grabs sunlight to power these chemical shenanigans

I am the green goddess, the soul of the natural world. In plant leaves, you find me in blobs (or organelles) called chloroplasts – minute factories producing the food that plants need to grow and develop. The key is a chemical reaction called photosynthesis: water is taken up through the roots and carbon dioxide from the air, before they are converted into oxygen and sugar-food (glucose, a kind of carbohydrate) in the presence of light.

My skill at absorbing light is what makes the reaction go with a swing. You see me as green because I absorb the blue and red frequencies of the visible light spectrum and reflect the green – leaves turn yellow when I break down in autumn. Plants are a food source for most living things. So it's only fair to say that I feed the world.

Photosynthesis: water + carbon dioxide + light → oxygen + glucose

- Chlorophyll "a" formula: $C_{55}H_{72}MgN_4O_5$
- Size of chloroplast: 0.01 mm x 0.003 mm
- Used as a food colouring (eg. in pasta)

Chlorophyll

Protein

■ Chemicals for Life

☀ This complex character gets its oar in everywhere
☀ A coded genius involved in most things in your body's cells
☀ Forms complex organic molecules, folded in different ways

I make your body tick over, marshalling chemical reactions in your cells, speeding up reactions (as enzymes) and allowing DNA to replicate. My long polymer molecules are made of combinations (sequences) of 20 types of amino acid, which fold differently according to their sequence. The instructions for making me are there in your genes.

Protein

Swedish chemist Jöns Jakob Berzelius named proteins in 1838.

● First described by Gerardus Mulder
● First Protein sequenced: insulin
● First insulin sequencing: F Sanger (1955)

Chemicals for Life ■

* An amazing molecule, the twisted original that can copy itself
* DNA is short for deoxyribonucleic acid
* Every single living organism contains DNA

DNA

Since the dawn of life, my coded information has allowed the living world to be built, maintained and reproduced. My pair of molecular backbones twist around each other in a double helix shape. When unzipped and read by molecules called ribosomes – with the help of Enzymes – I enable the proteins in your body's cells and their chemical innards to be built.

● DNA first isolated: 1869
● Double helix discovered: 1953
● Discoverers: J Watson, F Crick, R Franklin

DNA molecules in your body are repaired every eight seconds.

Carbon
Chemicals for Life

* The fourth most abundant element in the Universe
* The basis of life, it's stored in plant and animal tissue
* Organic chemistry studies compounds containing Carbon

I'm a shapeshifter, who can morph into many forms. You can't pin me down! I can be clear, crystalline, superhard, non-conducting diamond; or slippery, electricity-conducting, grease-monkey graphite; or atomic chicken-wire graphene; or smarty-pants buckyballs.

The key to my non-metal marvellousness is my amazing, multifunctional bond-forming, which allows me to link up with others of my kind in long hydrocarbon polymer chains. In this form I make up all organic matter. On top of that, as inorganic CO_2, I'm absorbed by plants, who use me for food, and dissolved in the oceans, where I'm put to use in the bodies of sea creatures. Eventually, I cycle back into the air when I am exhaled by animals or absorbed into the Earth when dead organic matter rots.

More often than not, I'm unceremoniously dumped in poo.

* Carbon in oceans: 36,000 gigatonnes
* World's strongest material: graphene
* Biggest exporter of graphite: China

Carbon

Nitrogen
Chemicals for Life

- This usually unreactive sort has a highly explosive sting in its tail
- An amazing fertilizer, but can pollute and poison water courses
- Nitrogen-compound ammonia produced in the Haber process

I'm a steady Eddie. Although I make up more than three-quarters of air, I keep to my own, hanging around in tightly bonded, twinned pairs of atoms. Although you won't normally see me making a fuss about things, I don't suffer fools gladly. My triple covalent bond is so strong that those who break it often create explosions.

I'm vital to a mind-boggling array of compounds – you'll find me in chlorophyll, DNA and protein. Since plants cannot consume me directly as a gas, most of them have to find me in the soil – and they're hungry for me! This is why, as ammonium or nitrate compounds, I'm spread on fields as fertilizer. I also lurk in the bottoms of drinks cans, in clever little things called widgets, put there because my tiny bubbles give beer a lovely head.

Antoine Lavoisier called nitrogen "azote", meaning without life.

- Chemical formula: N_2
- Percentage of N_2 in air: 78 %
- Discovered by: Daniel Rutherford (1772)

Nitrogen

Index

A

Acid	46
Activation Energy	88
Air	96
Alcohol	72
alkalis	48, 126
Alloy	103
amorphous	8, 126
Atom	26
atomic number	26
Avogadro's Number	40

B

Base	48
base metals	102, 126
Boiling Point	15
Brownian Motion	16
Bunsen Burner	56

C

Carbon	120
Carbon Dioxide	112
Carboxylic Acids	74
Catalyst	90
Chemical Reaction	82
Chlorophyll	116
Chromatography	66
Combustion	86
Compound	20
covalent bond	20, 32, 126

DE

diffusion	16, 126
disassociate	46, 126
Distillation	63
DNA	119
Dyestuffs	78
electron	26, 30, 126
electron shell	26, 126
Element	18, 22
endothermic	127
Enzymes	92
Esters	76
ethanol	72
exothermic	104, 127

F

fatty acids	74
fertilizers	122
Filter	62
Firework	89
Fossil Fuels	104
fractional distillation	63

G

Gas	12
Giant Molecule	34
Greenhouse Gases	115

H

Hydrocarbons	70

I

Ion 30
ionic bond 20, 127
Isotopes 28

LMN

Lavoisier, Antoine 4
Liquid 10
mass number 26
Melting Point 14
Mendeleev, Dimitri 22
Metal 102
Metallic Bonding 36
Mixture 21
Mole 41
monomers 35
Nanoparticles 38
neutron 18, 26, 127
Nitrogen 122
noble metals 102, 127
nuclei 18, 26, 127

OP

ores 100
organic chemistry 68
Oxygen 110
Ozone 114
Periodic Table, The 22
pH 50
photosynthesis 116, 127

Pipette 61
Polymer 35
Precipitate 64
products 82
Protein 118
protons 18, 26, 128

RS

Reactivity Series 84
reactants 82
Rock 100
salts 30, 128
Seawater 98
Simple Molecule 32
Smart Materials 42
Solid 8
solutions 128
solvents 10, 128
states of matter 6–12, 128
sublimation 14
synthesis 82, 94, 128

TU

Test Tube 60
Thermometer 58
titration 61
Universal Indicator 52

W

Water 108

Glossary

Alkali A chemical base that dissolves in water.
Amorphous A solid without order to its internal structure.
Base metals The most highly reactive metals on the reactivity series.
Bond The links between atoms formed by the interaction of their outer electrons. There are three types of bond: ionic, covalent and metallic.
Burette An instrument used during titrations to determine concentration. It is a vertical glass tube with a volumetric scale and a tap at its bottom.
Caustic A substance that burns skin.
Centrifuge A machine that uses rapid rotation to separate substance of different shapes or densities.
Concentration The number of particles of a chemical in a certain volume.
Covalent bond A chemical bond where two or more atoms share electrons.
Crystal structure A solid with an ordered internal structure.
Diffusion The process by which particles spread through a solid, a liquid or a gas. In gases and liquids, diffusion is helped by Brownian motion.
Dissolve When a solid mixes completely with a liquid, forming a solution.
Electron A negatively charged subatomic particle, found orbiting the nucleus of an atom.
Electron shell Electrons slot into certain fixed energy

levels around an atom, called shells. Only electrons in the outer shells interact with other atoms or ions.

Endothermic A chemical reaction that absorbs heat energy.

Exothermic A chemical reaction that gives out heat energy.

Internal energy The movement of atoms or molecules in a substance. Internal energy can be increased by heat, or excitation with electromagnetic waves (e.g. microwaves).

Ionic bond A chemical bond between ions, held together by the electrostatic attraction between positive and negative ions.

Neutron A subatomic particle with no charge, found in the nucleus of an atom. It's the heaviest part of an atom.

Noble metals The most unreactive metals on the reactivity series.

Nucleus The centre of an atom, containing protons and, in all elements except hydrogen, neutrons.

Oxidation A type of chemical reaction where a substance loses electrons.

Oxide A compound containing oxygen, formed in an oxidation reaction. Metal oxides are often rusts or tarnishes on the surface of metals.

Photosynthesis A chemical reaction, which takes place in plants: sunlight and carbon dioxide are converted into sugar and oxygen.

Glossary

Polar A covalent molecule with an uneven arrangement of its electrons, giving it a slight electrical charge at its ends.

Proton A positively charged subatomic particle, found in the nucleus of an atom. The number of protons an atom has is also its atomic number.

Radioisotope An unstable isotope, which is radioactive.

Reduction A type of chemical reaction where a substance gains electrons.

Salt Compounds formed when acids are neutralized. These ionic compounds can dissolve to release positively and negatively charged ions.

Solution A liquid mixture of two or more substances.

Solvent A liquid that dissolves another substance.

State of matter The state in which a substance is found at a particular temperature and pressure. There are three broad states of matter: solid, liquid and gas.

Surface tension A force between the molecules in a liquid that pulls them together – it allows bugs to walk on water without breaking the surface!

Synthesis A series of chemical reactions that result in a predetermined product. This process is used to produce chemicals industrially.

Vacuum A space empty of matter, found inside thermometers and in outer space.

Volatile A substance that reacts chemically with other substances.